COPYRIGHT 2019 BY FIDDLEFOX
CREATED BY CHRISTOPHER VUK AND PHIL BERMAN
COLLECTED AND TRANSLATED BY PHIL BERMAN
ILLUSTRATIONS BY GABRIELA ISSA-CHACÓN
MUSIC PRODUCTION BY MARC DIAZ

NO PART OF THIS BOOK MAY BE USED OR REPRODUCED IN ANY MANNER
WHATSOEVER UNLESS WRITTEN PERMISSION IS RECEIVED
ALL RIGHTS RESERVED

Thank you for reading our Australian Heritage Songbook. We created the Heritage Songbook Series to promote musical understanding between children, parents, and educators around the world.

We hope you spend many happy hours with the children in your care singing these songs and listening to the accompanying recordings at fiddlefoxmusic.com. There, you'll also find coloring pages and other printable activities for all the books in our Heritage Songbook Series.

We've also included color-coded sheet music so young instrumentalists can play and sing along. We recommend using colored rainbow bells that match up with our notation system, but you can also use colored stickers on piano keys or ukulele frets if you would like.

Happy Music-Making!

From the Fiddlefox

www.fiddlefoxmusic.com

TABLE OF CONTENTS

	PAGE	CD TRACK
HOW TO USE THIS BOOK	4	
WELCOME TO AUSTRALIA	7	
WALTZING MATILDA	9	1
BOUND FOR SOUTH AUSTRALIA	15	2
KANGAROO, SKIPPY-ROO	21	3
TABA NABA	27	4
WALTZING MATILDA (KARAOKE)		5
BOUND FOR SOUTH AUSTRALIA (KARAOKE)		6
KANGAROO, SKIPPY-ROO (KARAOKE)		7
TABA NABA (KARAOKE)		8

Australian Heritage Songbook

AUSTRALIA

INDONESIA

PAPUA NEW GUINEA

INDIAN OCEAN

CORAL SEA

● Canberra

SOUTHERN OCEAN

TASMAN SEA

G'DAY FROM AUSTRALIA!

Australia is the only nation in the world that is a country and a continent. Floating between the Indian, Pacific, and Southern oceans, Australia is home to many unique species of animals for example marsupials like kangaroos and koalas carry their babies in a pouch, while monotremes like platypus and echidnas are the only mammals to lay eggs.

Aboriginal people migrated to Australia 50,000 years ago and developed a rich culture deeply tied to nature. Dry desert covers most of the interior of the continent, known as the Outback. Near the oceans, you'll find greener areas and rainforests.

Europeans came to Australia in the 1600s and soon began populating the island's coasts with towns and cities. Today, Australia is a diverse country, home to people from all over the world.

Welcome!

Waltzing Matilda

Once a jolly swagman
camped by a billabong
Under the shade of
a coolibah tree

And he sang as he watched and waited till his billy boiled
"You'll come a-waltzing Matilda with me . . ."

BASED ON A MELODY BY James Barr
LYRICS BY Banjo Paterson

WALTZING MATILDA

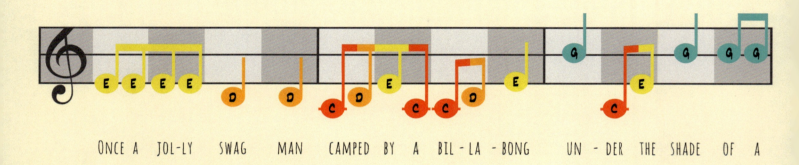

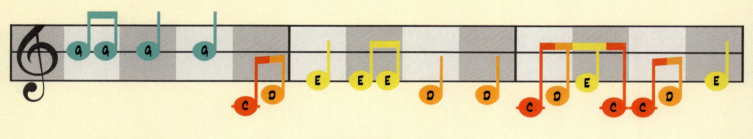

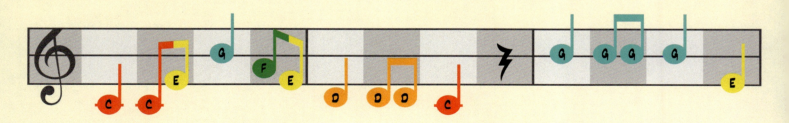

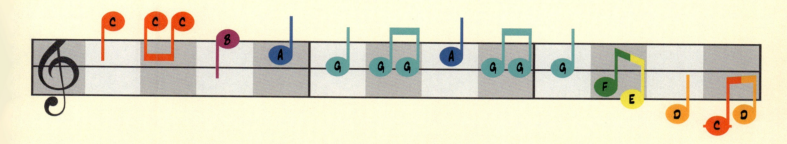

WALTZ-ING MA-TIL-DA, "YOU'LL COME A WALTZ-ING MA-TIL-DA WITH ME." AND HE

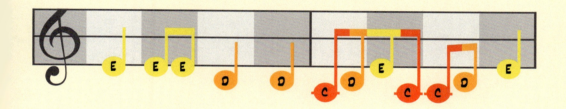

SANG AS HE WATCHED AND WAIT-ED TILL HIS BIL-LY BOILED,

"YOU'LL COME A WALTZ-ING MA-TIL-DA WITH ME."

BOUND FOR SOUTH AUSTRALIA

In South Australia I was born
Heave away, haul away

South Australia round Cape Horn
We're bound for South Australia

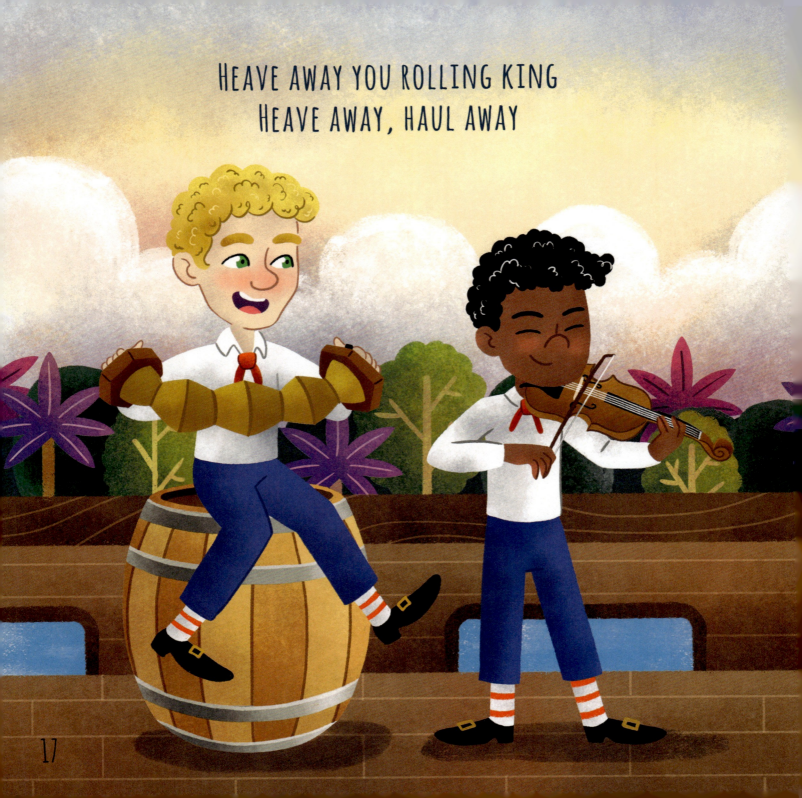

NOTES USED
C D E G A C

AUSTRALIAN SEA SHANTY

BOUND FOR SOUTH AUSTRALIA

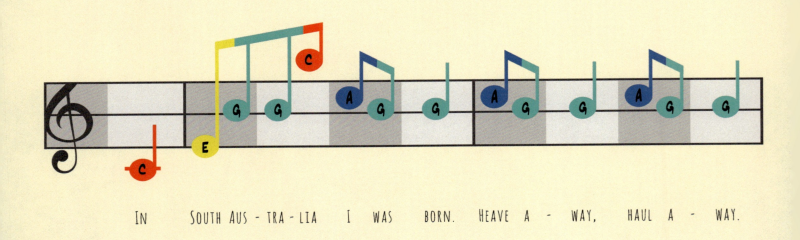

In South Aus - tra - lia I was born. Heave a - way, haul a - way.

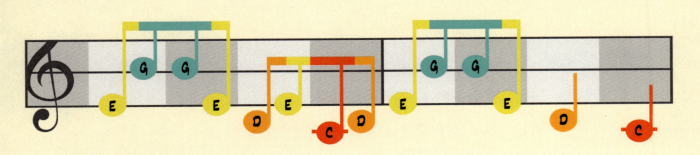

South Aus - tra - lia round Cape Horn we're bound for South Aus - tra - lia.

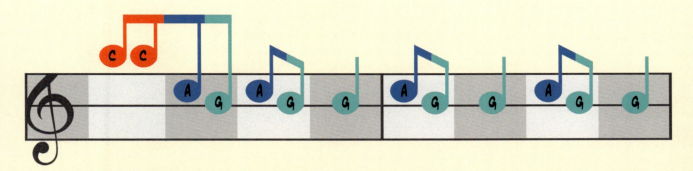

Heave a-way, you rol-ling king! Heave a-way, haul a-way.

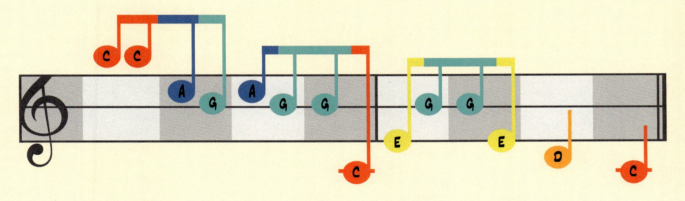

Heave a-way, oh hear me sing we're bound for South Aus-tra-lia!

KANGAROO, SKIPPY-ROO
KANGAROO, SKIPPY-ROO

Dozing in the midday sun

NOTES USED

AUSTRALIAN TRADITIONAL

KANGAROO, SKIPPY-ROO

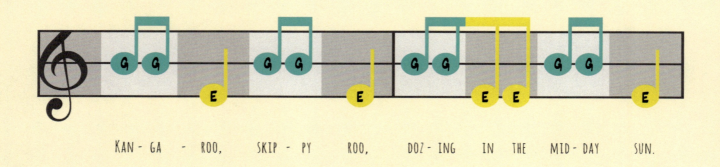

Kan - ga - roo, skip - py roo, doz - ing in the mid - day sun.

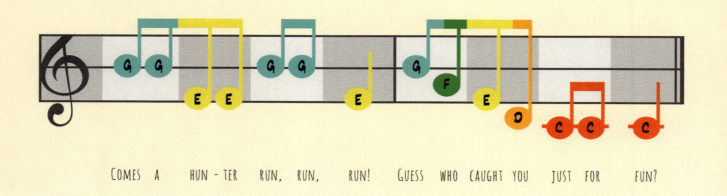

Comes a hun - ter run, run, run! Guess who caught you just for fun?

25

Taba naba to the reef!

Taba naba naba norem
Everybody go to the reef!

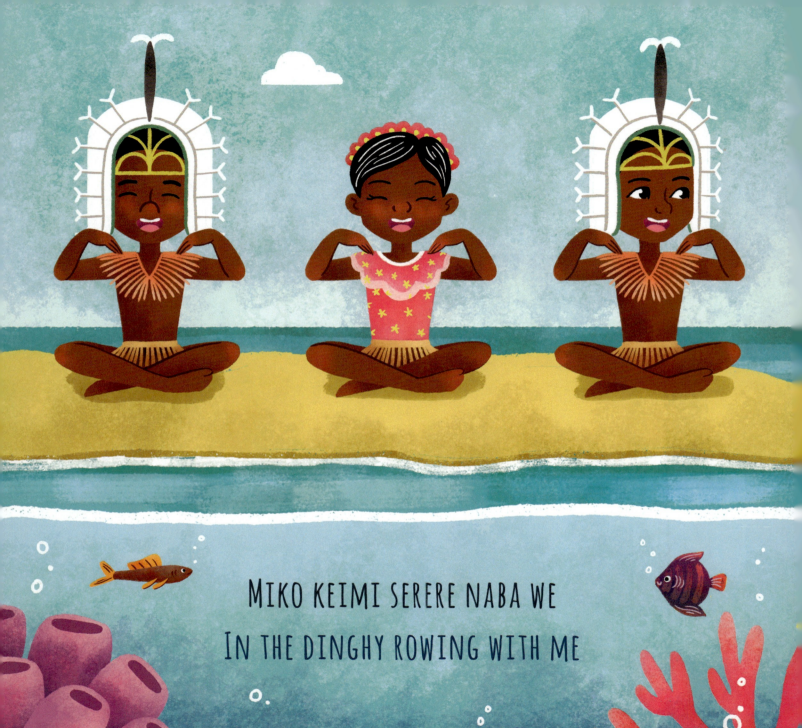

Miko keimi serere naba we
In the dinghy rowing with me

NOTES USED: C D F G A C

MERIAM MIR TRADITIONAL
FROM THE TORRES STRAIT ISLANDS

TABA NABA
TO THE REEF!

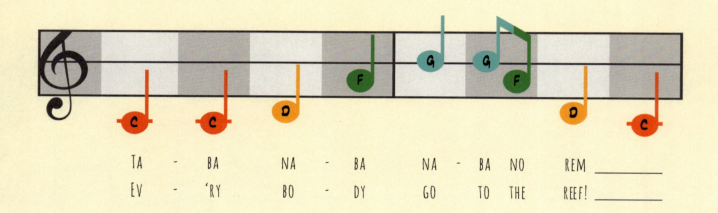

TA - BA NA - BA NA - BA NO REM ____
EV - 'RY BO - DY GO TO THE REEF! ____

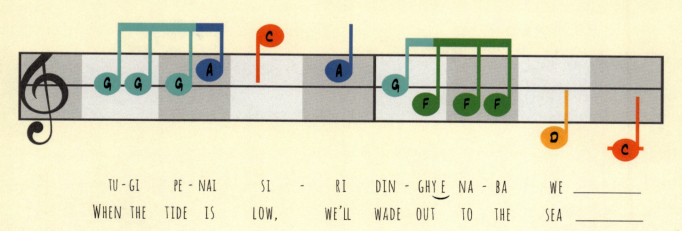

TU - GI PE - NAI SI - RI DIN - GHY E NA - BA WE ____
WHEN THE TIDE IS LOW, WE'LL WADE OUT TO THE SEA ____

31

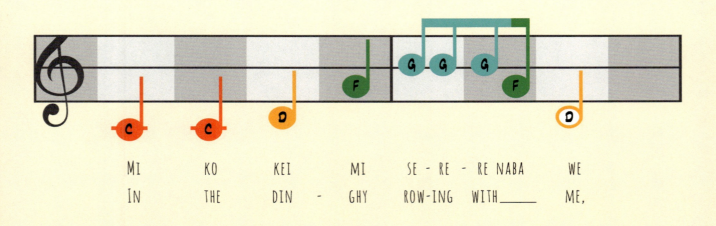